SADKO & SANTIAGO
WORMHOLE

2024

SADKO & SANTIAGO

LEIDEN

© 2024 Sadko & Santiago, Leiden
llustrations Willemijn Veenstra, Woubrugge
& Aleida van Zwet, Leiden & Tess Hubert, Voorschoten
Picture Merel Leijnse, Leiden
Druk van Sadko & Santiago
ISBN 9789464918007
First Edition 2024

CONTENTS

where the Muses go

drifters, lovers, enemies
and friends, of insect, stones
of snow and feather
feral entities, and little
bits in the huge cosmos

finding one another
in between the hands of time

the Calling of the Muse

Muse, take our pens & write
with your ghostly hands, shining, blinding alabaster -
take our throats & sing so prettily
of what presides over our minds.

we are two creatures, out of time -
out of that, & out of line -
we humbly wait, present

our problems, think & write
of that which always made us write.
we let you take our pens & write.
oh, lovely Muse, please write - do write!

the ink spills beauty blots,
we bounce back & forth our thoughts,
           here we write.
           we write, despite
           the page, ignite!

in a cabin in Quinnetuket

in a cabin in Quinnetuket
two figures sit
'neath deep red maple leaves,
'neath stars
'neath stones
falling like meteors;
they ponder

one slides a finger 'cross the creaking planks
and senses sparks of life;
of will, of care, of providence
the other 'knows' those sparks
come from the flint
lighting a cozy fire
in the cabin

while one provides the fire
finding soothing solitude
inside the flames
the other brews a simple soup
learned living in this cabin
in Quinnetuket for days, from all things
far away

they wander;
one through annual rings
it's witnessed growing every year,
nourished like its child, while the other,
the deserter, in the soil still,
in boots of war,
has felt and seen it all

one hesitantly seeking peace,
from gunshots free,
stumbled into the cabin
while the other, gently stirring through the soup,
seeks in silence; in its heart,
for feelings of reality, even the agony
that it's tried sheltering from

and so they sit
'neath stones falling like meteors,
'neath stars,
'neath maple leaves; with
what they care for in their minds
in search, in fright of other worlds
in a cabin in Quinnetuket

NATURE

Dialogue #01

the tree trunks twist and turn
the charrèd sky lurks from above
spirally, the northern winds churn
and raging clouds cover the sun
the rain pours.

– Hail, 't is Mother's love!
blessing us with this delight
such flawless sights she offers!

blowing out her deafening sounds
she rips a trunk out of the ground
a wandering deer is hit
it falls down stiffly

– Is this what her love contains,
this morbid scene?
– Morbid? Such a word obscene!
the contrary is true;
this scene is one of endless beauty.

thunder rolls and hurls a strike
to where a sudden fire lights
the raindrops sizzle in its sparks
shadowing the white-hot dark
and so, the weathers fight

– That beauty shelters in your head,
where all is well and dry.
we must not let her take our worth,
we must make the storm abide.
– Oh, let her go and overgrow!

and with a single thunderclap
the weather calms and slowly sighs again
and with it, time elapsed

– Look at the crops and at the plants
and at the animals that bloom.
while we were listening to ourselves,
she always, always knew.
– We live to see another day
and we reward ourselves
with the spoils that a victory
has brought to us.

and so, their wings burst out their backs
their bodies sectioned, armored, tacked
an antlion and mantis clumsily flutter
towards the azure sky

– You prance as birds will have you conquered,
I conquer the birds.
whatever beauty they may hold.
– Ah, such beauty that they hold.

Ode to the Mantis

Mantis! In thine habitat
that hides among the crippled leaves;
a Ghost, thou art, a Spirit!
spear that strikes and senses thieves

Mantis! By thine hunger
smite upon the silenced man,
rip thy barricades asunder!
tear him with thine Godly fangs!

Mantis! Pray thine prayer,
with thy patron sided, free
mimick every forest feature so, that
even Lacewings mimick thee!

Mantis! Shed thine skin
so that the crawling ones shall eat it
having traced thy trail exactly
believing to know how to defeat thee

but alas, thine fine surprise
thou mimickst thy true avatar
an overgrowth, a flowering grimoire
their utmost glimmering nightmare:
thine being without disguise

fly for now, Antlion

It
burrows
deep,
its head
sticking
inside
the sand.
Cowardly,
comfortably
waiting
hours
for
ants
to
fall,
having
them
devoured.

for now.
and fly,
multiply
only
they
provide;
Protect,
to
unable
insect:
for an
excuse
a sad
into
grows
it
So

the forest 'Everlasts'

I lie, limbs spread out in the grass
where leaves'd have fallen:
hazel, yellow, auburn, orange;
many vibrant hues of orange,
yet the autumn Everlasts.

I sit, my fingers tickled by the sticks
that would've carried crickets;
clicking, chirping raspily
beneath an elmwood canopy,
yet the lighter Everflickers.

I breathe the mid-september air
that charrèd acorns would enrich,
a scorching smell now overwhelms
and, smoking out my nostrils, welds
my senses shut; From Everywhere

I sew the spider webs together
in a last attempt to bind myself
to all the left-out fringes;
thin and subtle loosened fringes
yet the wisp did Eversizzle-
their flint now lights my lonely pyre-

(limbs far spread out in the grass)
deep in a long-forgotten forest
where the orange sky has crumbled
and the quiet cricket mumbles
and the only sound one hears
is my wire that Eversnaps

torn down

yes, that Everlasting forest,
once so green,
once so pretty,
forest floor covered by leaves
of every sort of bush and tree

I once went there, long ago,
with my grandpa, 'fore the war,
and he told me
child, you keep
this forest neat
and it will keep you too.

well, we didn't try at all,
no excuses to be made
we hacked and then we chopped
until all fruitful ground was paved

and this is Everlasting?
no, a new Highway's built.
and this is Everlasting?
no, a new Skyscraper's built.

try to find your sweet birds
in cement and in the glass
that we look through for a view
of a forest, lost in the past.

the fiery haze

the golden sunset's risen now,
the deep purple has faded
into a magenta blaze, from the unruly
azure to nighttime lazuli,
'tis now but a fiery haze

her luscious pines and junipers,
entangled trunks, and swaying oaks
and glistening as her universe,
enchanted caverns; Emerald cove
dissolve into your fiery haze

her diamond stars, so pure, inlaid
into the tranquil midnight sky
the crescent, Holy Pearl, is worn;
the moon her pavilion adorns
still, blistered by your fiery haze

she trod in all her elegance
and fought in her unrivalled craze
she pranced across the mountains,
leapt into her ice-cold lakes;
blown severed; ash in fiery haze

one day, I'll plant one severed seed
and pray a single, simple wish
more fruitful deeds alike will meet;
your highways overgrown with weeds;
your fiery haze extinguished

a hole in the clouds

the winter wind ravages,
through the streets
and through the windows

                            making umbrellas crack
                            while turning inside out

gunshots in the distance
a figure in the fields;
reaping what he sows,

                      a rag tries tearing off his neck-
                     fiercely pulling with the storm-
                            the figure shouts,

adjusting his scarf, stout and torn
heaving up the gun he wields,
he roars a challenge from below.

                 I, awestruck, watching from the balcony
                    shot a glance at yesterday's sprout
                        as it withered 'for my eyes

for a moment rumbled the mansion
as if ripped from its roots and
harvested as nature's yield.

his cigarette did slowly blow;

                    as, in that moment
             the figure, ragged and outworn,
              he shot a hole into the clouds,
              he fired harder than the storm.

the sky then tumbled, shocked,
and filling up with cigarette smoke,
it crumbled down.

                    it shattered as a
           heaven-covering plain of glass

and with a flick, he dropped himself,
smoldering,
onto the grass,

                      onto the ground.

the wind lay low,

                 and didn't get back up.

if nature was a king

if nature was a king
every grass-blade would be sharpened, shine,
the trees would wear a thousand rings,
the rivers would be filled with wine;

nature is humble, calm, unseen,
she's ambient and evergreen
and in her own, she is divine
a seamstress sewing threads so fine

with only some nights golden fur-

if nature was a king
we would not have poisoned her

the Birdwatchers

between the trees tall
and the leaves that slowly fall
I stand in the midst of it all

between the sky blue
and the ground so subdued
I stand in this land I've accrued

with this pair of binoculars
I watch the lens dirty and slur
the image, the wind hotly whispers

I see how the sparrows have fought
each other, plucking and pecking
and stabbing the others
'till their feathers fell out (their feathers fell out)

I see how the sparrows have fought
each other, cause keeping the peace
is a human invention, and territory
is mine, my hill (the one you must kill me on)

I see how the sparrows have fought
each other, for their beaks are sharpened
by the cockfight, their vocals hardened
by the stinging of their voice for days on end

one sparrows glides swiftly
on the wind's whisper
fleeing the other's bloody beak
attempting to gain some peace

the other sparrow chases him,
keeps ruffling his feathers
and pecking till the feathers
are red and dark and stiff

between the trees tall
and the leaves that slowly fall
I stand in the midst of it all

and I watch through binoculars
and the faintest of whispers
how the sparrows keep fighting
on their hills.

the mockingbird

I hear a bird from maple trees, its caws
are such a lovely song – its tender voice
and chest are frail yet still it makes rejoice
as winter winds blow and winter snow thaws

a mockingbird it was I think, that bird,
the bird that perched on branches young and strong
then even, still it sang its lovely song,
the wind too tried to make its cries unheard

the branch had looked so lovely under me
my wings had glided to a sudden stop
to sing my opus as I rested here

I sing so sweetly here for me and thee
and on the branch of maple tree I hop
morendo fading in the sunset clear

diary of a winter wind

there I went then. Gone was the wind,
and me with it – a spurt of breeze,
between trembling pine needles
and withering branches – to freeze

the tops of trees is an art form,
to sprinkle the leaves with ice
is a passion you keep with care,
dedication and spurts of nice-

ities are plenty and I am rambling,
the trees are overflowing
and dripping with snow. And yet,

I stay careless, desert the distance,
I am the wind and bring the cold
and to unknown fields I go alone

HUMANITY

Dialogue #02

in the lush-green parks
that sprout from seeds
carefully hand-planted
– Stands a gardener with a
mighty shovel,
ploughing through the earth

in the cemetery
quiet, engraved with
lingering reveries
– Stands a mortician with a
shovel of death,
uprooting those poor souls

in the Cathedral
with Heaven-reaching steeple;
cold walls engraved with hope
– Stands a preacher with a
towing robe and holy book
before his people
For he whistles at the skies
and feels connected
through its currents

in the palace
dreaded by the townsfolk;
yet held in reverence
– Stands a king who's built a
kingdom in this forsaken place
A king but pampered
by the people, that
formatted in line

the ridges covered gold;
the palace grounds, much
larger than the town
where poverty and famine roams

– Still, I see these different classes
be as one
in symbiosis
– In society!
you call this unison?
I witness chaos, mayhem!

a messenger comes rushing in
with papers and a dipping pen
the gates crash open
in a giant clowny grin

– A war will wage,
again! These foul beasts..
– though this war has been agreed upon
out of mutual necessity!
– They build their masterpiece in rapid fire
only to burn it to the ground
again,
right after

– They can but control themselves
as in the spider's web
every single one, as one
yet trapped in their mirage
of human silk

– Struggling as ants: determined and strong
– While conquering like demons

an ever watchful eye emits
from the horizon
as they bicker
they slowly shrink and petrify
in the same spot
and stick there

the Horse

there, beyond the dunes
(windswept into place)
there beyond the sea
(with her everchanging face)

there in the sky
in their audacious grace
rises the sun fiercely
giving warmth to all
as Apollo brings himself twixt clouds
and never lets reigns fall

but between that rumbling ocean
and the dunes comes a commotion

for the grains of sand are trampled
under hooves of pure white bone
as an animal comes hither
striding proudly on its own

the Horse, a beast of beauty,
as ferocious as the sun
as its counterpart the serpent
as persistent as the hum
of the bees, maybe more fitting
would be to name it wasp

for so persistently it questions
until its victim drops– but no,
that is too mean, that would do
this Horse injustice of the gravest,
its mane is rich with intellect
and feelings of the richest harvest

the Horse is proud and smart and kind
though sometimes rash
though sometimes blind
the Horse now graces this beach of yore
and may the Horse gallop for evermore

the beetle

up on a Horse, in saddle, sits
a fully crested beetle;
lance in hand, a worthy weapon,
horned and cloaked and truly regal

several decades, he has wandered
on his ever trusty steed, he'll
flee the land through miles of desert
a deserter, cowardly and feeble

hunted by the hivemind;
stealing Honey is illegal
with a lethal poison, leaking
on his sideways-pointing needle

so, he sucks the Horse's life forces,
be it like a mosquito—
and thinks of gold and ladybugs
entering the cathedral—

straight through the gate,
the sandstone crushed the parasite,
so evil

and the Horse around it swayed;
it's being quite
the quadrupedal

with its captor in the sand
and with its forces back in hand

it grows its wings, and freely
flies off as an eagle.

Castles in the sand

I would still watch
their young and innocent
fragile, limp hearts
on a thin thread of friction depend,

I would still tremble
while the stubborn little bastards
those defiant grains of sand
are blown apart,

I would still stand
amidst the dry and itching landscape
the meadow piled with pyramids,
laying betrayed in smoke, in faith,

I would still chart
the footsteps in the mud
drilled in with discipline
the wayward boots of wasted blood,

I would still listen
to the cheers of victory;
the howls of despair
wishing this Kingdom Come to be,

I would still travel
to this truth-forsaken land
to that long built up facade;
to the Castles in the sand,

I would still clench
those fleeting grains extracted
molded into crosses
along the road erected,

I would still dampen
my injured eyes
water this drank-dry desert
if it were to free my mind.

there were the Days

there were the days where blades crashed
into each other; cruelly slashed
the cheek of the other; bashed
heads in with the butt of their sword; dashed
forward in a ravenous fury.

there were the days where enemies battled
with anger in eye; where chainmail rattled
with each tired step; bloody wrists shackled
to the torn warships; [blank] laughs cackled
in the face of barren victory.

yet, after they cruelly cut
with, in cowardice, their red eyes shut
yet, after the guns had been stored away
for the night, once ended the tiring day

on the battlefield, they'd play
soccer (fußball, voetbal, sport au foot)
on the battlefield, they'd play
together (zusammen, samen, ensemble)

children again, five, six, seven, eight
years again, now fiend, now mate—

but Halt! Stop! Wait!
Mark this date—
of play! (of play?)
(once the blood is washed away)
(will we play again the next day?)

the bomb

set the blinker
of the bomb on
before you place it
where it hides
or you'll forget the spot
where it resides
and you Must remember
you just Must

run
run as fast as you can
once you've set it off
because only our top scientists
could disable the powder
from exploding
and by then you'll be dust
lost in the rubble
of the dangerous radius

so

Keep it safe. Keep away.
it's not yours to change.
the bomb will quickly
start ticking. If you do.

the Pigeon/the Rook

the darkened walls are stained
bricks stacked on bricks.

a sorrow Pigeon through the river wades
for the bridge, the city's spine, was bombed
but even the river is sick.

it sees a Rook is coughing
in the corner, cawing wronged
she wades on through the tar.

the riverbed feels rough;
it cuts her skimpy talons
punched to bluntness in this war

she struggles on
past factories and smoke,

her feathers drop increasingly
sinking further with every stroke.

a little 'for the shore,
its beak descends
inside black pages.

then, like gum from off the floor,
she pulls herself upon the shore
escaping from the ink of yore

the war it wages
in her heart,
from which her hope she took,

is like a wart,
it's sticking to her evermore

while she now sickly coughs
soaked black fully,
as the Rook

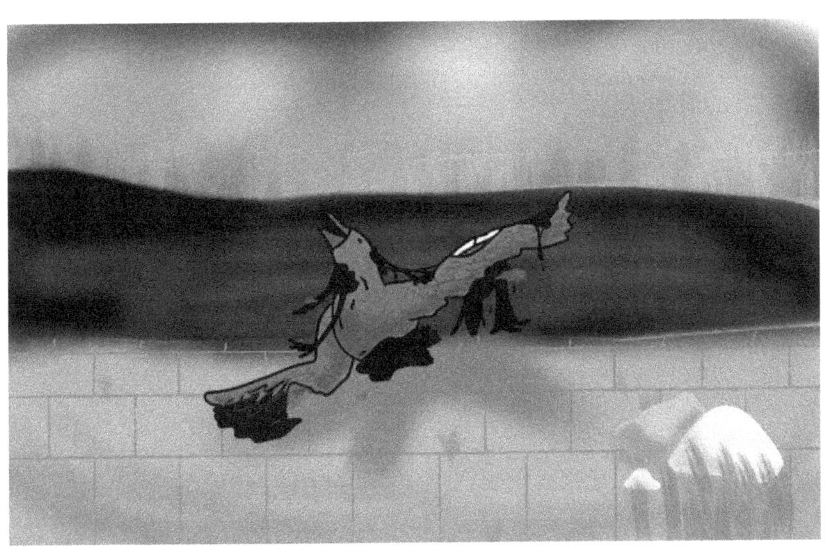

One and the Same

the swallows flew there,
when I was a swallow I flew
over the wind-worn peaks
of sun-beaten mountains.

the wind blew there,
when I was the wind I blew
over the jumping deer
of those rain-drenched forests

the circus rested there,
when I was a trapeze artist
I helped setting up the tents
and handing flyers out to innocents

the light dimmed there,
when I was the light
I watched through wrinkled fingers
how they beat the restless

the proud shed their guilt there,
when I was guiltless I watched
as they kicked the worn
and punched through the nearly born

the brave become cowardly there,
the humble become proud there,
the careful become careless there,
it all goes to hell there—
Where? Where? You ask tiredly, *Where?*
Where, with bags under eyes, you ask?

there, I point
and I point far enough
to point right back at us

we, the swallows,
we, the wind
we, the circus,
we, the light,
we, the proud
we, the brave

we are one and the same.
we are a circus, we are the blame
and the blamed. The shamed.
we are One and the Same.

migration

One swallow glides the smooth winds;
the delicate, western breeze
she caresses, softens its clouds,
tends to its atmospheric wounds
and then is softly carried down.

One swallow flies the fiery winds;
the burning easterlies
she learns to fight, inflicting draughts
and blow up any whereabouts
and claws her way towards the ground.

One swallow rushes pressing winds;
the booming southern reeks
she thumps and bashes, swirling up
in hurricanes, but she resists
and grips steadfast into the soil.

One swallow rides the frigid winds;
the grueling northern freeze
she clambers through the currents
with but talons and a will
spinning into recoil.

In the middle of the world
a sparrow quartet sits on branches
feathers ruffled, neatly tucked,
a polar blanket, nearly plucked
they sing of windswept places
birthing cities with their phrases

and they sit there, bound to branches,
bound to moon and bound to sun,
as bound to sky and waters run,
as bound to stars and stone
and bound wherever from,
we, birds, are bound in unison

fireplace (a lonely road)

I've walked a lonely road
a long and lasting lonely road,
and it's a barren, lonely road

the fireplace no longer burned;
my children, shuddering in sleep,
so to this road I have returned

I would have taught them cards all evening,
and sipped my midnight ale,
had snow not fallen through the chimney
in my hard-earned open hearth
making their faces scarily pale;

so now I stand, misunderstood
and chop my fury in the wood
and chop my fury in the wood

Mother, abandoned

well, think about it:

tulips forced to be tall, red, pink, blue —
the curve of the piano, smooth and hurtin'
linen woven to be a clean curtain,
plastic chairs and alloys, too —

is that not our legacy,
the steam engine's rust?
that depraved hunger, lust
for edges sharp and orderly?

like canaries, the men choke
and the women spoke
of ill will towards the child

the breath of the wild
has sizzled, dwindled
into a flame unkindled

of course we're filled with hate,
as they heatedly debate
if they'll kill us with sticks or stones;

of course we're filled with rage,
as they stick us in a cage
and strip us to our weak-willed bones;

but the grass never abandoned
us like we left behind ourselves;
as we renew in rebirth,
let us return to Mother Earth

love to all

o and yes,
the men slaving
in the coalmines
who came to beat
their wives at night
loved their Uncle Sam
and saluted him
of course

o and yes,
the women slaving
over white-hot stoves
who came to shout
at children dear
loved their Lady Justice
and prayed to her
of course

o and yes,
we the children
of a New Age
love our uncles aunts
and all who despise
our modern youth
of course

o and yes
we wear our powdered wigs
and dance a dandy jig
to the commie anthem
as we grin with rotten teeth
and we love our country
and its rotten people
Of course

jar of Honey

on the shelf in the kitchen
on the wooden creaking planks

there is a jar of Honey
a jar of glass, clouded glass

that lets you look from out
but blinds you on the inside

that is fragile yet deludes itself
to claim pillars of stone
rather than its columns of dust

that jar kept me inside too once
and when I broke it to get out
it splintered, burrowed into my skin,
bit, grasped, kicked, did

whatever
whatever to keep me in,

because we are all Honey,
Liquid Gold, Drink of the Gods, Human Ambrosia
maybe poisoned, maybe diluted,
but Honey still,

we cannot imagine
a life outside of that jar –
(how it would feel to roam
the kitchen and the house?)

we are Ambrosia in a
cage we could easily break

and that jar, it needs us
to think it's a vault
while its jail is faulty
with bars of bent brass
for it is just a jar
a jar of fragile glass

in Soil and Slate

I made, at my avaunted spot,
the sun inflame a warm embrace
and shadowed by an autumn haulm
I lie in love, afraid, amazed
I lie in Soil and in Slate

atop a hill, uplifted by
the furrowed earth, there nigh, I listen
to the unabashèd Cricket; --
its delicate arts on violin
its relished tones that shine so thin

the silken laces sing:
'You ought to lay away your boulders,
kindle up alive within—
let the left behind you smolder;
let the Currents take you in'

so I travelled, looking back
at cursèd wisp and smoth'ring smoke
a lonely firestone was stacked
upon the others, lost and broke
upon the many lost and broke

and I became a stone inlaid; --
another brick within the wall
the orange, laid in Soil and in Slate,
more orange than the fall,
was far too orange for the fall

DEATH

Dialogue #03

– and this is the Last Stop.
the last beating of the heart.
can you imagine to climb
onto that boat, your Last Depart?

the freckles on their face
are golden, almost elfish
yet their elfish face expresses
melancholy for their trees
and how the Riverkeeper
doesn't flinch for all the bees

a coarse hand, blistered
by the heat in the barracks
is brought through unruly hair
(how Mother loved that hair)
and blue eyes, dead eyes,
look at the golden coldly

– I speak of the dead.
you speak of the lifeless.

they laugh and they sound
like a muse, melodious and
otherworldly, escaping
every minute that they speak
(their golden freckles
glittering in the sun)

– is not everything dead
that was once good?
let us return and bring fresh air
into those holy lungs.
but death must come to all
each soul must hear that death song sung.

– of elks and of moose
of *those* lungs you speak
but of those that breathe around you
for *those* you dare not breathe.

the sun moves east
and the sky turns into the purple
bruises blossom into
after an hour or two
as the duo morphs into
a phoenix and a crow
morbidly awaiting
the Last Breath
that them must follow

sparrow sestina

a sparrow floats awake from out his nest
the morning shimmer chips away the sleep
he listens to his neighbors 'round him sing
and watches as they prance above the sky
as it lied yesterday, the mountain lies
and still as yesterday, the wind's a sigh

he startles out of trance and with a sigh,
he sulks in quiet, patching up the nest
he knows a storm, again, tonight, that lies;
the rumbling surely will disturb his sleep
and lightning will be crashing through the sky;
his little throat will not be warmed to sing

the sparrow hears the wind's opted to sing,
leaves that play the flute ruffle a subtle sigh
he mightily spreads his wings and mounds the sky
like no return abandons his own nest
he ponders on a thought that was her sleep
and drifts away in words of rest; her lies

he wanders off towards the grass she lies
in, remembers however she used to sing
she fell as if she tumbled down in sleep
and breathed as though her breaths were but a sigh
she lied upon his back, stumbling to their nest,
savored the final notes that sung the sky

he feels the weight collapsing from the sky
and sees how unstable his child-home lies
the branches rudely blown from out his nest,
a dirge is screeched, a bare attempt to sing,
the trees uproot with only but a sigh;
it leaves the forest silent, trapped in sleep

he's granted nevermore a good night's sleep
he stares up at the grey, cloud-covered sky
he heavily evokes a heartfelt sigh
and turns to where that single mountain lies
he meets a lonely star to which he'll sing
and with this sorrow tune restores his nest

the Dove, a sweet cycle

From a reaper's journal

I tread over the trembling bridge,
-the city's spine-
and looked down at the blackening river

there, dancing on the ridge
I watched, in colors ghostly coralline,
a Dove- in frightened shiver.

I held my hat atop my head
thus, shadowing my swindling face
the gun locked in its holster

the further in, lighter the tread
my fleeting footsteps, unerased,
the currents hastily cut corners

colder, grasping at my will;
my inhumane appearance;
tattered eyes and heavy breaths

I shift into the grassy fields, so still
I hold my thunderous interference
as I flick and light a cigarette.

the winter sighed at last, she quivered,
felt a gentle fingerbone;
and flew into the next-in-cycle: spring,
allowed the welcome touch of death.

correspondence

From the last email
Dearest john,

How have you been?

I know with the wife gone
and the children done
there's not much left to stay.

I know with your heart weak
and your lungs meek
there's not much left to stay.

How will you be?

I know what to tell you,
about that feeling blue
there's so much there, away.

I know how to tell you,
through a hand deathly true
there's so much there, away.

This is how it will be.

(how do I know,
you ask with a trembling lip
as you watch the screen lit
up with these harrowing words)

I know because I am coming,
your End is duly blossoming
and the flower of your life
will be snipped once I am there.
I have some great garden shears
I'll try out on your olden years
I've meant to try them— anyway,

don't worry, john,
about the emails you have yet
to touch. They aren't your business
anymore.
nothing is your business
anymore.
only my hand is your business
anymore.

so, john, I wish you the best,
for the rest
of your days.

My condolences and greetings,
Your Personal Reaper

what john sees
then the laptop screen
shuts off, turns black
and the blue that it emitted
disappears — the back

of john, his stomach, face
are tense and trembling
as he watches the screen
to see if something happens, anything

but nothing does. And so john,
at his office desk with splintered wood
rolls away in sleek office chair
and wonders what to do he should;

the Reaper is coming,
he knows,
it shows

(in the lip that trembles,
in the frown that resembles
Zeus's when he saw man first
come forth to wage war on Olympus)

the Reaper is coming,
but john tries not to mind
that it's his life that he'll miss
(if it's that end the Reaper comes to find)

maybe that end will be
simply a new beginning,
after the veil maybe will be
an eternity bone-warming (or chilling)

but john will find out,
knows he will know
when the hand of Death
appears 'fore him slow,

and the Reaper takes john
to that mysterious place
(if there's any at all
If there's anywhere to face)

to john at least
from what john can see
there's a beach? a forest?
a vague tapestry
of dunes, sand,
bushes, trees,

but whatever john sees
is hidden from you and me

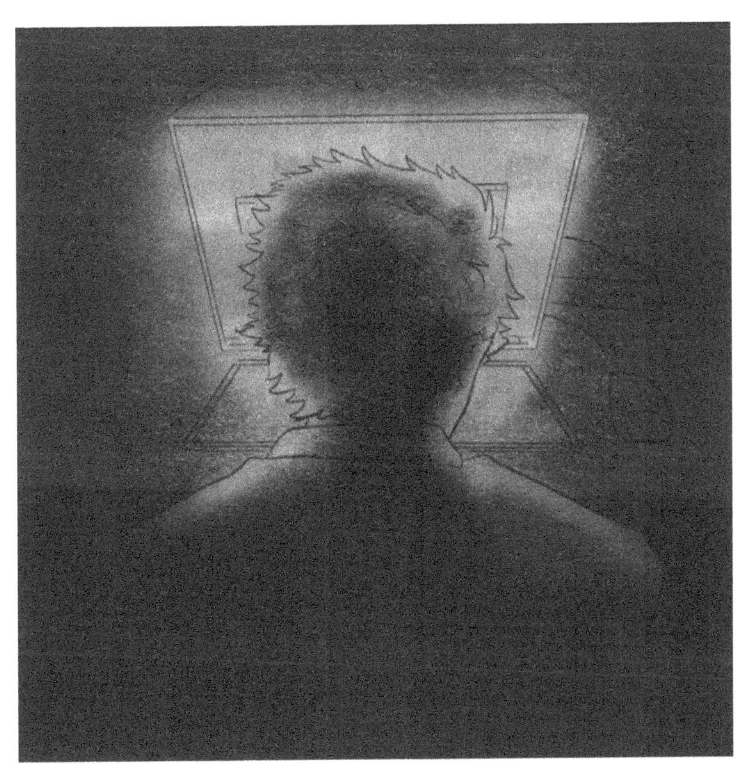

seagulls

Free at last!
I flap my sunburnt arms around
with purple shades atop my nose.
Odor of fishing boats that fills the air,
along with seagull sounds.

Stumbling out the yellow van,
I feel the shells beneath my feet:
the conches, clams and razors,
stabbing in my tiny feet—

while frolicking through the sand.

I play among crab-skeletons,
dead jellyfish and mussel corpses,
dancing in a ring with me,
all holding hands, all joining forces.

In my last fond memory
I was an old, content and finished soul;
ready to be reborn.

Yet now, I hear the rushing sea,
while running, falling, standing up,
and no longer am I forlorn.

nosedive

I'll never see that beach again;
the bright, blinding sun
that sets my dried-up skin aflame,
the sticky, clamped feeling of sweat
dripping and running down my back-

such a shame.

the monotone murmur of the sea
that follows my ears wherever
and plunges me into an endless, hollow pool
that wrings my lungs, filling up with water,
drowning, gasping, fading black-

oh, woe me.

I'll never step inside that van;
that yellow monstrosity, again
from which she looked upon the world
and failure sparkled in her eyes
with a smile, wide and unwise-

how unfortunate.

the seagulls squawk,
a dozen nosedives,
grappling her,

greedily,
they
tore
her
tiny
body
apart-

truly a pity.

mythic threads

a van drove by the greys last night;
a yellow one in fading wits,
reflecting the dull daybreak shine
ripping through speed limits

a measly man about six feet
with limbs as bones
and eyes as dewdrops meek
stepped out the driver's seat

he grabbed the sorry lump
from the yellow trunk
cut up in pieces
and he dragged the meat
as though it was his own

he'd sought their sewing services,
he muttered under shaky breaths
he pleaded them to sew her back in one
with mythic threads
their mythic threads

in a blink, yarn shot from ceiling, walls
from corners, nooks and crannies-
entangling her dismembered corpse
the kneeled man stared so desperate

I saw him lie outside,
his eyes now dry, no longer meek
and there was nothing there
nothing at all

I scurried away when
the scissors snapped
and in that moment, in his eyes
the world seemed at wit's end

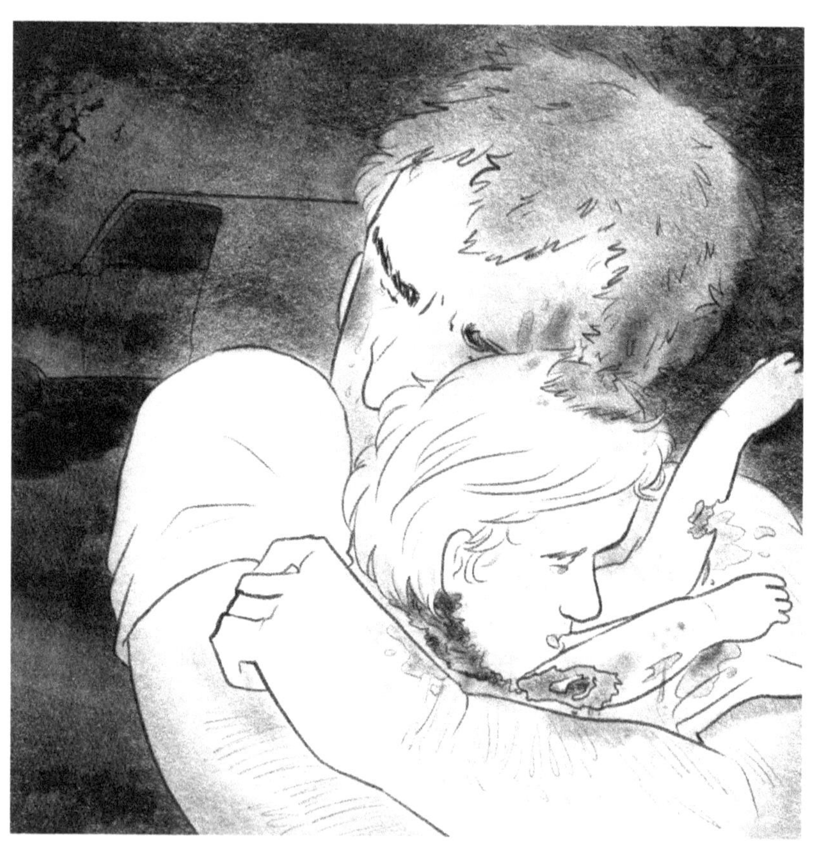

the three greys

she stood, silently
shoulders hunched
as she stooped
(her skirts all bunched)
over her embroidery

threading needle with
my yarn, a blistering red
the thread knotted looped
(her hands gnarled as they bled)
yet, true to the myth

next to her stood one sister,
her shade darker, almost black
with arms well-worn
(yarn held behind her back)
and eyes knowing, sinister

and the last of three
held a scissor pair
the pair which we so scorn
(wrinkled, rotten, with greying hair)
she held them out for me

and I watched as they snipped my thread
and I listened as they proclaimed me dead

Beware the Ferryman

I stride along a trail, obscured
by greyish mist and shrubberies
a dim and faded light illuminates
a sentence, carved in wood,
it read:
'Beware the Ferryman'

I'd ne'er seen such a sign before
so ominous and grim
it had me thinking
what if I'm already at the brim,
with my toes testing the waters
and my penny washed ashore?

the cobbled path shook for a moment
quiet was the next
wooden signs shot out the soil:
'Overall, you're all alone',
'Maybe this creek is the end '.
and 'Beware of the Ferryman'

I did not run for the woods,
I continue to this day
I will trip over a stick, over a root
before the bay

but I believe an isle's waiting
with a slightly brighter sun
where I pass into a painting
where my vibrant soul belongs

when I shake firmly Charon's hand,
and shall say 'thank you, Ferryman.'

wormfood

I could feel my heartbeat in my bicep
and it moved from muscle
to skin to nerve to organ,
pulling my body apart
and trying to escape me

I held it fast with two arms clasped
around myself, hands cramping
as they held my sides, begging
to stay alive. But what it wanted

it got. And so my heartbeat left,
deserted me in this hollow husk
and I had nothing to do but wait
for the ferryman to come get me.

I settled on the ground
body limp and one arm above my head
as if I were asleep. As if I
could wake up.

Instead of a ferryman I got nothing at all,
that boat never came, instead I felt my
eyelids close one last time,
my soul running after my heartbeat,
and I was left with nothing.

I got nothing at all
and nothing I'll keep
just my body frail
will adorn this ditch
as the worms come
for their feast

snowgrave

some time ago, I found a creature,
lying bloodied, stiff and cold;
it lied so absolutely cold,
my fingers froze, I felt a corpse;
a corpse walking the waking world—

as if on Winter's breath's behalf,
the hairs upon sandpaper thin
tried uprooting themselves,
revealing warm flesh underneath
my rashed and purple skin—

collapsed onto a coppice fence
beneath a frozen canopy
their bloodshot eyes wide open,
staring in the frost,
their red veins on the verge of popping—

heavily, their lips mumbled a sentence
(though I'd thought them frozen shut)
"the cold, it brought me revelations,
through the cold, I'll find my—"
after which, their jaw clicked firmly stuck–

that Night, I buried a pile of bones,
inside a grave of snow,
hoping that they may be relieved
to find their faith, and hibernate
in endless, wondrous Winter sleep.

FAITH

Dialogue #04

there the pages flew,
whispering in the wind
as they embark on a trip
from hands to dried-up river.

– none of it is real, you know.
we're real. that's it.

the other tilts their head
at the statement.
the sea is tired, noiseless
as it rustles against the sand.

– you think?
– I know.

the other looks back at the water,
sees the paper dissolve into salt.

– we're not.

now the one raises an eyebrow,
a skeptic made, not born,
and once he's quirked his brow forlorn
he questions other's words.

– how do you know?
– it's all out there. in the leaves,
in the trees, in the green
of the grasses of the dunes.
it's all there, there to see
for me and you. *can't* you?

the skeptic narrows eyes
at what's believed to be
a simple tide. it stays the same,
simply retreats into the water.

– if it's as clear to you,
as is clear to me,
the shells are just shells
and the sea's just the sea,
then I must be blind.

– blindfolded, maybe.
the other chuckles as they speak,
and look over at the skeptic
as the shells shimmer secretly
in the last rays of the sun.

– it's out there, everywhere.
you must take that cloth off your eyes
and grow to recognize
that which you seem so to despise—

– absent things cannot be hated,
the other claims, and crosses arms.

both are mute for precious time.
both are mute and say that's fine.
is this not what's fought for most?
the one laughs faintly at the boast
that It's out there, somewhere.
if It were out there, It would be there.

dusk has broken, the sun has gone,
the night now coming, dark has sprung,
the first stars of the night alight
the sky a little longer, but not for long,

for skeptic's laugh,
already chilling, turns into silver ice,
and other's mind,
always so willing, turns into pure white snow,
where does It go? how can they follow?

the Night

the tiles were cold against my feet
as I stood, basking in the moonlight
of the eve of wonders, eve and night
of miracles – none happened, yet

the fading stars twinkled, winking at
the poorest of souls that watched them (me)
and they disappeared behind dark clouds
as they watched sternly; silently

and there arose in me a feeling
quietly protruding from my chest
as poison ivy it creeped upwards
to claw at mouth and set forehead

this Holy Night was cold and freezing
the pure marble tiles were ice beneath
the cold then brought me revelations
and through the cold I found my peace

an Icicle

they stare intensely at the Icicle;
stiffly stuck in place
they feel its presence,
embrace its Cold,
its Sharpness in dismay—
their pupils locked away

they see the Freezing hook approach
slowly creeping closer,
a flash
its metal edge glistening so,
that it appears near magical
blinded by what must surely be
a Miracle

so welcome it with open arms;
they read it in the Book, they say
the Book,
protecting from all harm
the Book,
that glazes city tiles with an Icy coat
the Book,
which gifts misguided hope
the Book,
they read with their eyes closed

and as foreseen,
the stalemate's set,
predicted in their clouds of breath
a crack is heard,
the view is black,
and their belief will
be as though it's never been

they lie with open-piercèd head
their eyelids Frozen shut;
if only they'd,
themselves, had built
a furnace in their heart

the earth's cross

a great cold
Cathedral's
halls are grey
bricks on grey;
a cross the
fruitful land-
scape must bear for our sinful ways;
the sun comes up each morning, and
under bricks and stones, the earth so
sickly groans for all the murdered roots
crushed un-
der pious
foot. the preacher
in his dirtied
muddied robes
claims the Lord
loves each soul
that's trampled
under sinful foot.
what about those
You crushed,
O father, when
you built this
building so? what
do you know of
God? what do
You know?

Book; Roots; Leaves

the Book has withered in this form
the pages torn; the binding broken;
the Book's cream paper's lost its soft
touch; the ink has faded; a storm

has ravaged this poor copy here
and taken out its holy words,
but in the trees the paper grows
with words the same and just as clear

the blessings now live forth in Roots
in size and twist of foretold miracles
the blessings now live forth in Leaves
that cover the words' lovely fruits

old Sequoia (a lonely road)

I've walked a lonely road
a long and lasting, lonely road
but it's my favorite lonely road,

towards Sequoia, kind and old
I took my lightest, largest rug
and went to picnic in the cold

I'd drunk with her hot, steaming tea,
she'd told me long-lost histories
we'd written endless poetry
had I not there, fallen asleep

when I awoke, I felt the freeze,
I heard no rustle in the breeze,
yet she appears still in my dreams
yet she appears still in my dreams

the mist

I reach for a further grounding
in a mist of vagueness

with humbled paws
I reach for the "almighty"

but there is
Nothing
&
Nobody
in that mist

the fog conceals
simply more fog,
water condensed;
not even the water
is Holy

there are only my paws
pricked by thorns
of those who believe
that these swamps hold the key
but they are not here
there are only my paws
feeling and finding None

the one in the mist

and forth,
a slender silhouette
wanders in thick fog
rocking ever back and forth
and back

and forth
its black eyes ooze
and lengthened claws
swing back and forth
and back

and forth
it gulps on holy water;
spits it on the floor
wavering back and forth
and back

and forth
a twitching grimace
which Gods mocks
a cage itself has forged
and back

and forth
into a pile of sludge
it morphs, We watch
as it succumbs and poured
in black

and forth
and back
it rocks, chaos galore
and forth
and back

and forth

...

drawings in car windows

in a storm of white,
crushing that flurry underfoot
socks soaked with water,
melted from its picturesque image;
the water is like ice
as it sits in her lace-up boots

shivering in her boots
she stares at the car window; white
and freezing, the glass covered by ice-
cold snow, like that here underfoot
and in her mind she contorts an image
as constant and stagnant as the water

rampant as the water
under the ice and in her boots
but in her thoughts there floats the image
of a person – or a dream, light and white
as that which cracked beneath her underfoot
that restless fragile ice

on the car window, in the ice
the picture forms in frozen water
as the snow on the window and underfoot
feet uncomfortable in their boots
the girl draws a picture white
a beautiful ideal of an image

but as the snow is erased, the image
shows what is hidden; behind the ice
and in the car something hides 'twixt white
and black, a horrid grey, the water
melted and cold and leaking from her boots
and she's horrified, flattened underfoot

by this feeling, and the girl is pressed underfoot
like a flattened can; for behind her lovely image
she sees the terrible form, in her boots
she shivers in fear and in cold, the ice
had blanketed this reality, but the water
has given way and she faints, she saw– WHITE

white plains

she drifts in purest white, in void, in feud
so piercing, soothing to the skin
she floats in perfect solitude
her waving limbs steadfast, yet slim-

she's closed her eyes with lashes long
as wisps they flow beside her-
in her fading mind, a childhood song;
her pictures laced on wire.

there, daunting up from nowhere,
walks a silhouette, she knew once trusted;
it meets her in a faceless stare –

her slender body cracked, up thrusted;
she believed her bedtime tales, where
'Nothingness' existed, and she touched it.

an Ibis's love

when the morning left a hollow skull
and the dewdrops shined a little dull,
the woods grew faster than the day
and Ibises flew in straight array

I kneel down on damp surface ground
and tilt my head up at the Sun
and feel the rays in thousands count;
I spoke to Her, was shortly gone

then, all my worries disappeared
my head floats lightly like a feather
ascended, merging with the weather;
purest anger, joy and fear

she told me I should love the people;
fly above the highest steeple
shout over the mighty towers
feel my birdlike features flower

and with what little love is left
I'll love Her at my very best

from up above the Heavenly Clouds

From up above the Heavenly Clouds
the thunder tumbles down
loudly stomping on the pavement
outside.

Up atop our Holy Canopy
the hardy tiles lie aligned
one of them broken free,
with a crash, on the pavement
outside.

the Wings of Steel churn
emitting toxic fumes
they burn, and too, they make us burn
sauntering towards them
every day, step on the pavement
outside.

The Almighty Flame erupts
inside the core, the furnace –
coals forcefully shoved
inside the monster,
threatening those poor
and innocent on the pavement
outside.

The Fresh and Bright Outside
how we wish to be and breathe,
on the flip side of the agonizing brick,
and how we hope some Prophet
helps us flee from stained defeat
but hope's a futile thing.

Though our faith is rarely scathed
on our pavement, safe and thriving, deep
inside.

(we'll be arriving soon, my dear,
I promise it this time)

outside the Clouds

outside the Clouds
the molecules don't bunch up
frozen in the cold

but are free, darting around
hitting each other with a
Ferocity
a Ferocity only children possess
and mean, mean men.

outside the clouds
the molecules don't bunch up
frozen to nature's mold

but are free, a hassling crowd
hitting each other with a
Simplicity
a Simplicity only children possess
and ignorant women.

outside the clouds
the electrons hop

from hydrogen to oxygen
to nitrogen, and they laugh
as they make their way

from hydrogen to oxygen
to nitrogen, and they laugh
as they fly further still away

(my darling, we are molecules,
kept in the mold
kept in the cold
my darling, we are molecules,
Mean and Ferocious
Mean and Precocious)

the molecules wander woefully
once they've jumped too far,
back into a mold of their own making,

in a mold of pressed paper,
in a mold of fits and shaking,
in a mold of a burnt out star.

but for a fleeting moment
the molecules are free
and they feel the Sun on their protons
and their neutrons and electrons
and all their quarks and bits and bobs
and for a fleeting moment
the molecules believe the sun is spotless.

in a flat in Quinnetuket

in a flat in Quinnetuket
two figures sit in fabricated silence,
'neath plaster ceilings
'neath flick'ring lamps
'neath neighbors
with voices like gunshots;
they wonder—

one quirks their antenna,
jumps but settles once again
into the rocking chair from goodwill;
both sit in blessed comfort,
the other chuckles at ones nerves
from the linoleum floors,
knowing the doorbell had never worked;

their knees hurt from that late growth spurt,
(still the caps feel like rocks)
buckling as they stand;
the other does the dishes,
their hands cramping as they
listen to the
music of trees growing;

the music, the noise, the silence
has played for long enough;
the one sheds their feathers
black as ink on the couch,
the other gathers them up again,
their bold and brave feathers,
and makes itself anew,

and at last, their forms return to
the simplest air – the elf opens the door,
back from white, says a few words of grace
as the gnome, shrugs on its green coat,
replacing its coat of silver,
grins at elf and goes,
out of the flat in Quinnetuket.

and so they split,
'neath neighbors with voices like gunshots,
'neath flick'ring lamps
'neath plaster ceilings; having
found that other world, those treasures
and with more strange gold in mind,
in a flat in Quinnetuket

Acknowledgements

Thank you to Wouter de Jong for being so enthusiastic about this project and aiding us with every step of the way.

Thank you to Yolanda Bloemen for her expertise on the publishing industry and to Kinan Aldaioub for his expertise on self-publication and on writing poetry.

Thank you to Tessa Hubert, Willemijn Veenstra and Aleida van Zwet for illustrating our poems.

Thank you to Merel Leijnse for taking our picture.

Illustrations

About the Authors

Sadko and Santiago are both high school students and they love writing, music and cats. They live in Leiden.

www.ingramcontent.com/pod-product-compliance
Lightning Source LLC
Chambersburg PA
CBHW041206150726
48006CB00016B/2141